To Jan and Mike

TAKING STOCK

T G Carter *T G Carter*

*The Bard of
Windmill Hill at
Warwick Folk Festival
2014*

Windmill Hill Publishing

Also by Trevor G Carter:
Diamonds in the Desert
Children of the Fire

All Rights Reserved

ISBN 978-0-9557426-2-0

First published 2013 by
Windmill Hill Publishing

Printed in Great Britain by
www.direct-pod.com

Contents

Love and Lust

Notes from the Holiday Blog

Earth Matters

Looking In

Miscellanea

Contemporary Comment

Love and Lust

If You and I were Dragonflies

If you and I were dragonflies
　our love would be intense.
We'd make love on a lily pond
　or on a garden fence.

We'd do it with our wings tucked in
　then do it with them out.
And we wouldn't really mind too much
　if people were about.

I wouldn't need to go to work
　to earn a daily crust.
A dragonfly has but one thought
　and that one thought is lust!

The lust he needs to satisfy
　as often as he can.
In this respect a dragonfly's
　a fundamental man.

You wouldn't need to clean the house
　or cook us lovely meals.
You could wake up every morning
　then just do what appeals.

So if we were both dragonflies
　life would be simplified
by revelling in the bounteousness
　that nature would provide.

Poker Love

Lay your cards upon the table!
Don't clutch them to your chest
I want to see your labels baby
They look different from the rest

I've had enough of playing poker
I'm getting tired and it shows
I can't control the jokers
Who laugh at old Romeos

Most players play for safety
No one wants to open up
It's all bluff and bluster baby
And nobody gets enough

We all deal with what we're given
We make the most of what we get
Now I'm desperately driven
And you are my best bet

I need to raise the ante baby
To flush out any fakes
I need your hand to save me baby
As I ratchet up the stakes

For you're a diamond in my desert
And I feel your heart is true
So come on, let's form a loving club
I've got love in spades for you

We could fabricate a full house
And pretend we're kings and queens
Then we'll play happy families
In the back of limousines

Baby, life's one big casino
Everybody's playing tricks
But with me as your amigo
All our tables will stay fixed

Now I've shown you all my aces
And your king awaits his queen…
So lay your cards down on me baby
And cut yourself into my dream

Beneath the Bonnet:
the love song of Jeremy Clarkson

To turn you on I never need to plead,
my sweet protection from the wind and rain.
How you service my egotistic greed,
doing as I ask again and again.
Accelerator, dream generator,
You cocoon my soul in your sleek, tin skin.
My motorway mater, nothing's greater
than your fuel induced adrenalin.
Oh strap me to you, let us be as one,
then transport me to where all highways end.
Surround me, protect me; let's get it on,
my lover, my servant and closest friend.
Please reciprocate from beneath your bonnet.
Say you're turned on by this racy sonnet!

Love Train

If I'm pressed for an expression
  or asked to name a name
then a train of thought will lead me
  to state my sacred claim.
Let's look down on the demons
  we've mercilessly slain
from the safety of our idyll
  where we've so often lain.

Let's look at them and mock them
  from our defended frame.
We had to somehow stop them
  before they left us lame.
Now they're rotting in some valley
  of long cast-off remorse
while we continue skyward
  on our star-studded course.

When I was a wayward spotter
  in search of the right train,
sustained by vain imaginings
  of the love I hoped to gain,
I was without a compass,
  a map book or a chart,
assumed forever lost as
  I had a hollow heart.

Then you pulled me in your station
  with the force of your express
and transformed my situation
  with your glorious excess.
So when I'm torn and tattered,
  bedraggled in the rain,
bind up my battered ego
  and heal me once again.

And when the tracks run uphill
  and I am lost and lame,
then fire my spark of courage
  to reignite my flame.
And when the world of madness
  has burdened me with pain,
then fill your cup of kindness
  and dispense it once again.

She Did Not Know

She did not know that she had left him dead
and she did not look back once she had flown.
Yet her parting had snapped his final thread.

Though he had trod where others fear to tread,
he was careful his feelings were not shown.
She did not know that she had left him dead.

How could she see inside his tortured head?
How could she hear his deeply stifled moan?
Yet her parting had snapped his final thread.

His deepest thoughts were always left unsaid;
his inner feelings were a great unknown.
She did not know that she had left him dead.

He made her unhappy and so she fled,
feeling she would be better off alone.
Yet her parting had snapped his final thread.

Although he was clever and so well-read
he just could not face living on his own.
She did not know that she had left him dead,
yet her parting had snapped his final thread.

Compulsive Love

You only wanted to be loved, Love.
You didn't want to give it too.
You couldn't feel or see, Love,
that love I had for you.

You kept saying it was me, Love,
while I kept saying it was you,
as we never could agree, Love,
on what was false or true.

Although we felt we were in love, Love,
love itself was left outside.
There was no way love could win, Love,
however much we tried.

And yet I still call you Love, Love,
though we know that makes no sense.
As we were never in love
It was all a vain pretence.

It was a love that never was, Love,
although it wanted to be so.
It was a mockery because, Love,
we just put on a show.

The term's a relic of that lost love,
Something I cannot explain.
It's a remnant of the cost , Love.
Love can drive a man insane.

First Love

They say you never forget your first love,
and I know well what they mean,
as I can still recall mine vividly
though I was just fourteen.

We would disappear together
to enjoy our special time,
and though some said that it was wrong
to us it felt sublime.

She would soak up my youthful energy.
We could go for hours on end.
She was my glorious obsession
and my every weekend friend.

I knew when I first met her
she was the one for me.
If you'd seen us both together
then I'm sure that you'd agree.

I was convinced she felt the same.
And though she didn't say that much,
she communicated well enough
by fondling my crutch.

Then even when I chained her up
she still seemed to understand.
I felt it gave her pleasure
to meet my wild demands.

We'd commune deep in the countryside.
Oh how we loved the great outdoors.
Each time I took her for a ride
I'd forget my boring chores.

I've never met another lover
who let me do just what I like.
That's why I still remember her:
my faithful three speed bike.

The Attraction of Opposites

If you and I were antonyms
  then which words would we choose
to build a bridge between us to harmonise our views?
They say we need our opposites
  to make ourselves complete.
But if we dwelt on different planets how could our bodies meet?

Would we use some inbetweeny words,
  some conciliating phrase,
that drags us from our ramparts and by implication says
don't speak of Mars and Venus
  or of the far-flung stars,
for the distances between us won't heal our inner scars?

Would we speak of earthbound compromise
  and our cultural communions,
the lessons of the strong and wise, the joy of carnal unions,
the niceness of the everyday,
  the norms we hold in trust?
For as passion has its shades of grey there are limits to our lust.

And while the poets and the novelists
  exaggerate our state,
we find that in the real world common language shapes our fate.
So if you and I were antonyms
  perhaps we'd find a way
of meeting in a neutral space with softer words to say.

Notes from the Holiday Blog

Bankend Cottage

The wet, windy weather we weathered last week
made us yearn for the sunshine we set out to seek
at our holiday cottage in north-west Lakeland.
But good holiday weather doesn't come on demand.

Still we made the best of that north-west frontier,
Going out for short walks, hoping rainclouds would clear.
And though they persisted, we persisted as well
looking out for a sign of a brief sunny spell.

We played Scrabble and Boggle and avoided cross words
and observed many species of visiting birds
as they came to the garden to eat nuts and seeds
whilst we studied the book that identified breeds
and explained all about them and things that they do -
and now I'm writing this I remember a few.

There were chaffinches chomping around on the ground
while an impeccable woodpecker made a tick-tocky sound
as tits twittered and wittered in a language unknown
while a solitary sparrow scratched round all alone,
perhaps waiting for others of his common kind
and though they failed to turn up he did not seem to mind.

In addition to these ornithological thrills
we viewed distant vistas and tramped up some steep hills
where we scanned panoramas so splendidly vast
they reminded us sadly that nothing can last
except maybe the mountains and the presence of rain.
And we left feeling we'd like to come back again.

Mr Hogg: the full story

There we were in our tent so snugly and warm,
when my wife did lament in the eye of a storm
"There's a noise getting louder. I think it's a rat
that's come into our tent, and I'm worrying that
it may get in our pyjamas and cause us distress.
And I think it's a problem you ought to address."

At the thought of a rat coming in for a feast
I thought the only good rodent is one that's deceased.
My wife said "Get the torch, and find out if it's true!"
So, as a man's gotta do what a man's gotta do,
I did as I was bid and fiddle-fumbled the light
to expose the dread beastie disturbing our night.

Yet I found not a rat, nor a dog or a frog
but the beady bright eyes of an ageing hedgehog.
So I said "Mr Hogg, you must vacate this tent.
I don't welcome intruders who cause wives to lament.
You should not have called at this hour of the night
and I'd like to you leave now, if that is alright.

I concede you look smart in your spiky old jacket,
but my wife wouldn't like you. She just couldn't hack it.
I'm preferring your presence to a cat or a dog,
but please wander off now and find hedges to hog,
or ledges to lurk on, or cracks to attack.
I urge you to leave now and not to come back."

Well, he looked quite alarmed; dare I say, more than I,
As we both held our gazes and stared eye to eye.
And when I grew tired of this sterile stand-off
I reached for a stick and emitted a cough.
I had decided to act to defend our abode.
Mr Hogg sensed the fact, it was then he strode –

well, it was more of a shuffle and a rapid retreat,
as he knew it was hopeless and conceded defeat.
But as intruders go he really wasn't that bad
and once he had gone then I felt almost sad,
and went back to my bed thinking thank goodness for that.
I would rather have hedgehogs any night than a rat.

The next day I wrote down all about Mr Hogg
and featured his visit on our holiday blog.
I recorded my thoughts and my wife had her say,
then we put on our hats and went off for the day.
But much later on (yes, you've guessed it alright)
Mr Hogg reappeared in the deep dead of night.

Knowing that it was him by the sound that he made
I thought, last night's invasion is being replayed!
And how dare he return to disturb us again?
Was my message not clear and sufficiently plain?
So I crawled out of bed to locate my old torch
which I'd put in a pouch by the tent's entrance porch.

And then I found him there, just as bold as before,
at the site of our previous night's no-score draw.
So I fumed and I swore and I got very mad
and said "Why have you ignored that stern warning you had?
And how dare you return at this hour of the night?
What's your justification? What gives you the right?"

He said "Forgive my intrusion. But I've babies to feed,
and my good wife insisted I come back and plead
for a bit of your surplus to help us get by."
And as Mr Hogg pleaded he'd started to cry.
My gaster was flabbered to hear the beast speak -
an oratorical hedgehog! Is he some kind of freak?

Is this really happening or is it a dream?
Sometimes we can see things that are not what they seem.
I questioned my senses, I puzzled and frowned,
then I gathered my thoughts and defended my ground
saying "Am I your keeper? Do you think this is fair?
Please leave us alone now; we've got nothing to spare."

And then something happened that you would not believe.
But it's as true as this story, for I would not deceive.
Mr Hogg spoke again; words that melted my heart,
for this was the message he had come to impart.
He said "But if you were hungry, then what would you do?
Can't you see every man is an animal too?"

At this proposition my feelings flip-flopped.
I beheld my dilemma. Time seemed to have stopped
as it dawned on me that Mr Hogg had a case
and my dismissal of him was a dismal disgrace.
And I felt so light and joyous as I changed my mind
that I apologised to him for being unkind.

I said "Forgive me, forgive me! Now I've seen the light.
No one should go hungry. That can never be right.
It was clearly a sin to treat you with disdain
and now I must thank you for making it plain
that we are all mere mortals who should share what we've got.
I must think what to give you, though we've not got a lot."

I asked "What kind of food would your wife like the most?
We still have some left-over bits of old toast."
He replied "Oh come on now, do better than that.
After all, I'm a hedgehog! Not a dirty old rat!
A nice cup of fresh milk would do nicely for me."
I said "You're out of luck mate, we're both dairy-free.

But we do have some organic pure wholemeal bread."
He said "Oh that'll do nicely. I'll have that instead."
Then I gave him a few other odd bits of food
whereupon he retreated with his spirits renewed,
and I returned to my bed after playing my part,
grateful to Mr Hogg for my strange change of heart.

Postcard to Devon

Oh land of luscious wholesomeness,
Mecca of the creamy tea,
how effortlessly you impress
those visitors like me
who commune with your fecundity
and romp around your hills,
and venture in your viscous valleys
to taste your earthy thrills.

How we revel in the fulsomeness
of your dairy of delights,
your clumpy lumps of plumptiousness,
your milky chocolate nights.
You are a feast for all the senses,
your charms I can't ignore.
However much I get of you
I'll always yearn for more.

And as I've felt intensely close to you
On this magic, moist weekend,
I'm writing you this postcard
that I don't know where to send.

Earth Matters

Taking Stock

There are various reasons why we mess up the seasons
and we know well what these reasons are
as we live for the play that we're playing today
it is plain that we aren't thinking far.

As we begin to recoil from the high price of oil
some argue that we should fly less
for climatic disorders that don't respect borders
are causing all kinds of distress.

Now the world's heating up there's less water to sup
and the systems just fail to deliver.
While in places they're fracking for the fuel that we're lacking
as the locals all shudder and quiver.

Scientists get together to talk about whether
the weather is getting too hot.
Though they try to sound clever it seems they can never
reverse those sad graphs that they plot.

So it's left up to us to curse and to cuss
and come up with a credible plan,
and though our heads ache it's for our children's sake
that we change little things where we can.

We can insulate houses and wear thicker trousers
to reduce our dependence on oil.
Those who don't want to shirk can all cycle to work
and spend weekends tilling the soil

on those patches of ground that we see all around
between the closed factories and shops,
those allotments of hope that can help us to cope
with the rising demand for clean crops.

Not the fertilised fudge supermarket men judge
that we all want to eat more and more of,
but good organic crops, sold in our local shops,
that we so like to chew to the core of.

It helps us to feel grounded, despite being surrounded
by fast food and corporate excess,
to search for a stance that will give us a chance
of usurping a little bit less

from those gifts of the earth that we've known since our birth
and yet always have taken for granted
as we're in for a shock if we fail to take stock
of how the seeds of our future are planted.

The Earth Inhales

John Betjeman concluded his poem 'Slough' with the lines,
'The cabbages are coming now;
The earth exhales.'

The cabbages are dying now.
  The earth inhales
the poisons we have fed to it.
  Our system fails.

Our system fails to take account
  of its effect.
As man has failed to trim his sails,
  the earth is wrecked.

The earth is wrecked upon the rocks
  of our excess.
We're running short of vital stocks.
  We must use less.

We must use less consumables
  we can't renew.
Or take our chances on the rocks –
  including you.

Including you, including me –
  if systems fail.
The cabbages are dying now;
  the earth inhales.

Recycling: a fantasy

When my recycling days are over
I guess I'll be recycled too,
my bits broken down to sediments
as Mother Nature's bound to do…

perhaps to feed a sunflower
which in turn will turn to seed
for someone like me to devour
to satisfy a primal need
and by such means to start again
becoming part of someone else
to share their joys and share their pain
by this organic act of stealth
then I'd cast my subtle influence
and they'd cease to be free
when I use them as my instrument
to be yet another me
and disguised by my recycled state
I'd become myself and more
as my spirit would regenerate
from my seed's immortal core.

This is the best that I can hope for
when my recycling days are done;
that I too can be recycled
and once more become someone.

The Earth's Muse

Now they are digging deep inside my skin
for bits of my body they want to burn.
And I'm feeling we can't go on like this.
I am thinking that they will never learn
as they are digging deep inside my skin.

When they gaze upon my great unspoilt parts
I hear them exclaiming "How exquisite!"
Then they carry on the same as before,
oblivious until their next visit
when they gaze upon my great unspoilt parts.

And that's why I erupt from time to time;
to remind them all that I have feelings
and that actions have their consequences.
There are always limits, boundaries, ceilings;
and that's why I erupt from time to time.

I can feel my temperature is rising
as their activity goes on increasing.
They don't realise they're playing with fire.
If they stopped to think, it's not surprising
I can feel my temperature is rising.

For a long time I didn't mind them here.
In my Ice Age days when I wore deep snow
they mostly lived and died without much trace.
Way back then they didn't disturb me, so
for a long time I didn't mind them here.

I gave them everything that they needed.
But they abused it as their course was set
on so-called 'progress' and 'development'.
And now they've lost their respect for me; yet
I gave them everything that they needed.

Now they are digging deep inside my skin.
And though I've been here ever since my birth
they don't seem to notice that I'm alive.
I am Mother Nature. I am their Earth.
But they are digging deep inside my skin.

Planted

We didn't ask to come.
We were planted here
in bags of blood and fat and bone
to be bemused receptacles for the fear
and ignorance that we have known.

We are confused.
It's not surprising.
It takes time to make sense of it all.
But now the temperature is rising
and it seems we're riding for a fall.

We didn't ask to come.
But it's where we are,
and it's really quite a special place.
It's been good to us, this present star.
There's nothing better out in space.

We are confused,
There's no denying.
That's why we've done the things we've done.
And now we find ourselves agonising
over how our web can be unspun.

Looking In

Books you have to put down

Some people love books with an enthralling plot,
  the sort of thing that is hard to put down.
But I prefer books I put down a lot;
  that make me think, or puzzle or frown;
yet, at other times, make me laugh out loud
  at the madness of our human condition;
that make me question the furrow I've ploughed
  and see life from a different position;
or that make me weep at the hurt we impose on each other
  as I lament on our history's excess;
or that inspire me to think that we may yet recover
  from the horrors of our self-imposed mess.

There are many books like this that I love
  to put down again, and again and again.
And these are the books I treasure the most:
  ones that can help to make living more sane.

Khalil Gibran, Simon Schama, James Fenton, Thomas Hardy;
  wit and wisdom to enlighten our path.
How I love to keep on putting them down
  to imagine, to weep, or to laugh.

Starting and Stopping

How do you get started?

I write out a first line and I try to match it.
If the next line looks fine, then I will attach it.
Once I have got started, I won't be defeated.
I'll continue until a quatrain is completed.

A poem has purpose, this tries to explain it.
I feel once I start that I have to sustain it.
It provides satisfaction to show I can do it.
So I keep on going until I get through it.

Though it's hard to decide where a poem should end.
If you go on too long you can sometimes offend.
Perhaps that may suffice on the subject of how?
If I've written enough, I think I should stop now.

To the Last of the Letter Writers (never to be sent)

for Ralph Sheeran

I am waiting for your final letter,
the one you wrote before you died
in order to avoid the horror
I suspect that you would not abide.

Not for you, that sheltered housing
insulated from the wild night skies;
not for you, a dependent life
surrounded by sad stifled cries.

The gracefulness of your demise
becomes the memory that you leave;
your privateness, your curiousness,
that inner world no one conceived.

Is this where letter writing ends,
when a receiver can receive no more?
And who now writes letters anyway?
We've all forgotten what they're for.

Though I think perhaps I shall still write
to you sometimes if I feel in the mood,
and you'll read them in your gentle night
where no distractions can intrude.

The Ballad of the Missing Vicar

This is a true account of my mother's funeral on 18th July 2012.

The vicar was late for the funeral!
Such things shouldn't happen, I know.
But the vicar had let down the party,
so we had a late start for the show.

All the mourners were looking confounded,
and some of them started to pray.
While the sponsors appeared astounded.
What will the Almighty One say?

The pall bearers had hoisted the coffin
and they were clearly raring to go.
But oh where was that C of E vicar?
No one at all seemed to know.

The undertaker went off to phone her
as something was clearly amiss.
He said "I can do it myself if I have to."
We thought "We're paying good money for this."

(I had written a rude line at this juncture
then decided I'd not put it in,
as it spoke frankly of bodily fluids,
that in this context, I feared, was a sin.)

The times we are in are peculiar
and there's little on which to rely.
But vicars aren't ones who should fool you.
Just recalling it all makes me sigh.

When people ask if it all went off nicely
I suppose I will say "Oh yes thanks",
and not mention the C of E vicar
and her strange chronological pranks.

She had forgotten to check in her diary
regarding when we had planned to begin.
And although she appeared regretful,
that did not atone for her sin.

She arrived just before we got started.
Then things went off much as we'd planned.
We bade goodbye to our dear departed,
as she left for that far-away land

that she always believed she would get to
on the day that her number was called.
Though if she was looking down on that vicar
then I'm sure she'd have been quite appalled.

Yet when the proceedings were over
the mourners said it was all worth the wait,
overlooking the embarrassing issue
of the vicar who turned up so late.

The Self-Storage Option

I took myself to a self-storage warehouse
to lock up my troublesome side.
There's a part of me I find hard to live with;
though please, believe me, I've tried.

I'd been having some big problems lately,
and there were things I could not reconcile.
I'd tried being soft, then hard on myself;
then I tried going into denial.

Then I said "Look! I can't go on like this.
It's a struggle maintaining the show.
And the upshot of my analysis
is that one of us has got to go."

So I discussed the self-storage option
and I agreed that I'd give it a try.
Then I prepared my bad half for adoption,
though the plan brought a tear to my eye.

I'd been living with me for a lifetime
and it was the only life that I knew.
But I'd decided this was the right time
to escape from all the stress I'd been through.

So I presented myself at reception
and spoke of how I would like to be stored.
The clerk thought I intended deception
and suggested my idea was flawed.

Well, he needed a lot of convincing
to accept care of the worst half of me.
But after a great deal of persuasion
he reluctantly accepted my plea.

Now I'm feeling much better without me,
since mothballing my trouble and strife.
And I recommend the self-storage option
to those seeking control of their life.

The Domestic Request: vacuum cleaning

I have a keen interest in pedantry, although this can get me into trouble. Sometimes it causes stress in a relationship. For example, recently my wife said "You should do more of the housework. Why do you never do the vacuum cleaning?" I said "I can't do that. It's impossible." She said "Impossible? Why is it impossible?" I said…

You cannot clean a vacuum
because there's nothing there.
There's nothing *in* a vacuum,
not even any air!

A vacuum cleaner cannot do it
nor can any known machine.
Vacuum cleaning is impossible
as a vacuum's always clean.

The term is an oxymoron
as it fails to make good sense.
So I suggest you do not use it:
There's no logical defence.

Miscellanea

Longtrowel Erections

By rapid erections in which you can trust,
  Horatio Longtrowel earns his daily crust.
If you need a wall up, then he is your man.
  So give him a call up to discuss your plan.

He's a natural mixer, he can do it by hand.
  He'll risk any contortion to meet your demand.
He's fast as a ferret and knows every trick.
  He is the bricklayer who smart people pick.

He's a phenomenal worker and does what he says.
  Where it takes others weeks, he'll do it in days.
He lists commendations as long as his tool.
  He's handsome and witty and nobody's fool.

No job is too small or too big or too silly.
  His long trowel keeps working when winters get chilly.
No hindrance deters him from getting it up.
  He only drinks tea when you give him a cup.

He's heroic by nature. Horatio does it best!
  He exceeds expectations as his tool never rests.
Don't risk other builders who won't do it right.
  Horatio can keep going for most of the night.

Horatio Longtrowel – remember that name!
(Once he's serviced your needs you'll be glad that he came.)

*PS I have a sideline as Horatio's agent. Please get
in touch if you have any building work pending.*

History of the Word 1

When long ago the first life stirred,
was it the chicken or the egg?
We do not know what then occurred
for they left no recorded word.

Then words were written down in ink
to represent our human thought.
And this provided us a link
which proved our ancestors could think.

And when the tree of knowledge shook,
somehow, our history began.
Recording thought was all it took
to instigate a sacred book.

From sacred books to pop and porn,
the words were used for vulgar means.
A media machine was born
which treated sacred books with scorn.

As sacred books just gather dust
lost in the nooks of our neglect
our culture is consumed by lust
and we don't know which words to trust.

Now messages are sent by text,
communicating instant thought.
The sacred books have lost respect.
Nobody knows what's coming next.

History of the Word 2

The earliest books were all handwritten
by scholar scribes in meticulous hand
as the common folk were not yet driven
by a need to escape ties to the land.
And their role in life was so circumscribed
that they ploughed their furrows with little fuss.
If required to write, then their cross inscribed
compliance; although that seems strange to us.
So the written word expanded slowly.
The literate class, a separate breed,
were then mostly made up of the holy
men; who assumed commoners had no need
to express themselves in recorded form.
Serfs weren't asked for their opinion.
They were concerned with keeping fed and warm.
The world of books was a foreign dominion.

History of the Word 3

"Where there is no vision the people perish"
Proverbs 29 v18

As technology extends its hooks
the West forsakes its sacred books
and heedless of the time or place
succumbs to digital embrace.

While in the East the righteous chant
enchanted words they know can plant
a certainty in those who hear
who'll then transcend their worldly fear,
as they brush off the rough caress
of materialism's crude excess
and seek things that cannot be bought
in any Western style resort.

Conviction is a vital spark.
Without it life is just a lark.
Beware the coming of the night
without the books that brought us light.

Which-doctors

Which-doctors of the modern age
tell modern man how to engage;
which things to watch, which things to eat;
what we should do to feel complete.

They issue edicts from their screens
that form our hopes and shape our dreams
and help us choose which which to woo.
That's what the new which-doctors do.

Witch-doctors in the times long gone
were sages who worked out what's wrong.
You took your problems to be solved.

It seems a shame how it's evolved.

Contemporary Comment

**No Sex Please, we're Bishops:
a judgement on modern theology**

Oh pity gay C of E bishops
who're denied natural bodily fun,
and must stifle their God-given urges
before they have barely begun.

For they must abhor gay liberation
wherever it strives to exist.
And when it comes to their sexualisation,
the policy's clear: you resist!

They're not told that their urges are sinful
but to act on them's going too far.
Which seems quite a queer kind of logic.
Are we not, after all, who we are?

The celibate life should be celebrated
in the eyes of the C of E God,
while the rest of us think this outdated,
and denial of sex, rather odd.

It's not as though such activation
would make any difference to us.
Why should sex between consenting adults
create such an Almighty fuss?

Three Lessons: Huhne v Price

Big deal maker, fornicator
  Obliterates himself in style
Trades his wife for younger model
  Seems in love with his own guile

Wife publicises dodgy dealings
  Schemes to bring the big beast down
War of words and bitter feelings
  Mr Big hands in his crown

Wife ignores the consequences
  Thinks she can escape the rap
Pins her hope on weak defences
  Gets ravelled up in her own trap

Three lessons of the sad, sad story:
  Vengeance is not always sweet
  A pyrrhic victory brings no glory
  Some fights are best kept discreet

Shivering Tits

I have read that birds are collecting cigarette ends to line their nests.
They have somehow realised that the filters contain insecticides that
have the effect of protecting their dwellings from infestation.

When the winter comes and the deep cold grips
please spare a thought for the shivering tits
and give your fag ends to construct safe nests
that those creepy-crawlies won't infest.

It's fags they need, not just birdseed!
If they could speak then they would plead
for fags to make them feel secure
and help their babies to endure.

So please help out our feathered friends.
They're not as bird-brained as we think.
They know they need our old fag ends
to keep them feeling in the pink.

Their lives are not at all like ours.
They really do not have a lot.
Yet birdies have instinctive powers.
They make the best of what they've got.

So when the winter comes and the deep cold grips
let's keep our scarves, our hats, our mitts;
but give our fags to the shivering tits.

A Last Address to Mrs T

And so, goodbye, old Iron Lady -
usurper of the royal we.
Although essentially illiberal
you used your handbag liberally
as you pursued your regal mission
to make our nation great again,
while digging chasms of deep division
and claiming you could heal through pain.

Dismisser of post-war consensus,
derider of the nanny-state,
believer in robust defences,
dispenser of cheap mortgage rates:
your legacy is all around us
though some will mourn and others rage
as they all argue in your shadow,
dominatrix of the modern age.

The Stye in our iPad

This is a comment on news of a suicide epidemic in Chinese factories,
where workers are paid as little as 30p an hour to make Apple products.

There is a stye in Apple's eye,
They're pretending to ignore it.
Their precious image is on trial,
though they're trying to restore it.

Now, some of us may heave a sigh
who have iPads and Players.
We need our fix for getting by,
so don't have a lot to say as
it is a problem far away
in a land of low horizons
where workers slave for little pay
while we play with the prizes.

There is a label for this game:
it's called 'Globalisation'.
And we're all fixed into its frame
to fuel its generation.
We are all pigs penned in its trough
afflicted by myopia.
And none of us can get enough
as we build our dystopia.

We all have styes within our eyes
but prefer to just ignore them.
We pander to our corporate ties,
while in theory we deplore them.

Electrosmog

This smog we cannot smell or see
controls us all ethereally
through microchips which sense our touch
that have become that vital crutch
by which we all exchange our views,
seek out our thrills or check the news,
or advertise the things we sell,
or read the latest kiss-n-tell.

Life is one long electric slog!
Some do their texting as they jog,
fixing up the next arrangement
of their electrified engagement -
decide the time, agree the place,
then add that little smiley face
that always looks good at the end
to say you're everybody's friend.

Some even log on on the bog
to keep up with the latest blog
or flog their rubbish on eBay
or plan a weekend getaway,
or hook themselves into Facebook
to make more friends who'll maybe look
at pictures that they put on show
to demonstrate they're good to know.

Because you can, you often do
slog through the smog as it needs you
to justify the Wi-fi way
that snogs us while at work and play

as we worm and squirm within its web
all wishing we were that celeb
whose latest exploits grace our screens
to show what success really means.

Yet there are those who still hold back
against technology's attack;
eccentrics who contest the case
for Wi-fi in every public space.
They claim this electrocuted life
creates more trouble, toil and strife
by demanding much too much attention
to pointless updates and invention.

As the silence of electrosmog
invades our culture like a fog,
those who attempt to stand aside
will get an ever harder ride.
Yet technophobes can feel complete
without the need to text or tweet
and communicate their latest thought
about the weather, news or sport,

or the latest iPad or download
or super software to decode.
And they often go for weeks and weeks
without a glance at WikiLeaks.
Some of them don't log in at all.
They defy the electrosmogic call.
But it matters not that they resist
as one day soon they won't exist.

When all our lives become connected,
all electronically infected,
and we're all servants of machines,
all serving time glued to those screens
which will record each daily dealing,
our every thought, our every feeling,
will anybody think it strange
and perhaps attempt to disengage,
and looking round at what's remained, ask
has more been lost than what's been gained?

Enduring Wit

I do sometimes lament the death of wit
when I behold the comedy of our time,
thinking not much of it is truly fit
for purpose. And if our culture's in decline,
why is this so? Is it an ageing thing,
or are we running out of ideas?
And I wonder what the next wave will bring.
But fashion goes in cycles. It appears
if we wait a while things may get better.
A cliché? Yes, but history proves it's true.
Most of those we label as trendsetters
are just reinventing stuff we used to do.
It's a comfort to think when things are poor
that history, in time, provides a cure.

Advice to Claimants

At the Ministry of Surplus Capacities
the surplus souls stand in the queues,
waiting to sign on the register
to attend their ongoing reviews
which find them some more forms to fill in
and make them think of what more they can do
to convince us that they're really willing
and deserving of dosh that is due.

It's not an inspiring occasion,
attending these temples of doom
where officials suspect there's evasion.
This all fosters the feelings of gloom.
So, although it's a hard life for workers,
it's still better by far than the dole;
as the public like shunning the shirkers
whose lives are bereft of a role.

It's best, if you can, not to go there -
but if fate should dictate that you do,
don't try to work out why life's unfair,
just smile while you wait in the queue.
For we're all prone to being the victims
of forces beyond our control.
Just don't blame yourself if this happens.
Don't dig if you're thrown in a hole.

Ode to the Occupiers

Bless the ones who take a stand
Against those who destroy our land
And question what is being planned
And see it's not benign.
But pity those who cannot think
To read between the lines of ink
And barely swim before they sink
Into long-term decline.

Pity those who never learn
And stand in queues to take their turn
To borrow funds they can't return
And dig in deeper debt.
Pity those glued to their screens
Who always live beyond their means,
Addicted to their soapy scenes
And courses others set.

Pity those who are unemployed
Whose way of life has been destroyed
By something they could not avoid
And yet still have a go
At redefining who they are
While wishing on a tarnished star
And covering their inner scar
And going with the flow.

Pity those who can't escape
A life of economic rape,
Who cannot get their lives in shape
Or pass a simple test.
Pity those who think they're free
By being a celebrity,
By basking in banality
And end up just depressed.

Pity Facebook's generation
Who seek fake friends in desperation,
Complying with their degradation
Through their soulless quest.
Pity those without a hope,
The overwhelmed who cannot cope,
The cast adrift without a rope,
The terminally oppressed.

Pity those who seek romance
Yet never dare to take a chance.
They watch celebrities who dance
But never dance themselves.
Pity them and pity us
Who see all this and curse and cuss;
Who could, but do not make a fuss
Because we do not care.

But bless the ones who take a stand
Against those who destroy our land
And question what is being planned
And see it's not benign.
Bless those who say enough's enough
Who sometimes call the tyrant's bluff
And don't kow-tow when life gets tough
But paint a warning sign.

Bless those known as the occupiers
Who challenge all the corporate liars
And act as modern-day town criers
Denouncing what's malign,
Whose occupation makes us think
Why all that's good appears to shrink.
And as we hover on the brink
They paint their warning signs.

In the Big Tent: the thoughts of Big Chief Osborne

At the pow-wow in the big tent
  Deep in deepest Downing Street
All the big chiefs gather gaily
  Get together, feel the beat!

Toffee noses jaunty-jaunty
  Big Society on course
Make the plebs all work for nothing
  Steely hard times, no remorse

Give out honours like confetti
  Cheer the nation, rule divide
Mega sports day celebrated
  Media circus well on-side

Sporty-sporty Boris Blue Bike
  He excite the Tory squaws
Making Cameron bit nervous
  Boris him make sign - up yours

Chiefy Clegg he grumpy-grumpy
  Cos the Lords' tent still intact
UKIP banner rumpty-tumpty
  Maybe fishy for a pact

Gather-gather farmers, sailors
  Say to leave the EU club
Find the clitoris of the party
  Nigel, he know where to rub

Not afraid of Millibeany
  With his big brave Bully Balls
Chanting message of one nation
  Won't be long before it stalls

Battle on to next election
  Beat the drum for more the same
Bash the plebs and lower orders
  They the peoples best to blame

We no tax the smarty high-class
  In the mansions of the land
Look after those who know the system
  Sacred law: says feed the hand

Feed the hand that feeds the party
  Look after peoples just like me
Ride around in flashy Rollers
  Captains of our industry

Tax the spare space of the scroungers
  Load of bloody riff-raff scum
Wasting time in TV lounges
  While we do what must be done

Glory Glory Hallelujah
  Second term is bright in sight
Slay the Liby-Demy faction
  Then march further to the right

The Tale of Count Titticumcum:
the greatest storyteller the world has ever known!

(The best stories have no ending.
  They just pause, then start again.
They disappear, then reappear.
  And that's how they remain.)

Once upon a time…
There was a count called Titticumcum
  Who was an evil man
And like all evil men before him
  He hatched an evil plan.

When he arrived upon an island
  From his homeland far away
He found a land of opportunity
  And decided he would stay

And build a storytelling empire.
  And oh, what stories he devised!
And his empire grew and grew and grew
  And no one was surprised.

To help him organise his stories
  He employed a wicked witch
Who had flaming locks of bright red hair
  Ah, she was a feisty bitch.

And they recruited fair young maidens
  Who took off all their clothes
To titillate his happy readers
  So they'd cast off their woes.

Yes, they sent for comely maidens
  And the comely maidens came.
They all came for Titticumcum
  Had promised wealth and fame.

Oh, they built a glorious empire.
  The biggest breasts were in the Sun.
And he saw off his competitors
  Who all envied what he'd done.

He'd become the News Lord of the World!
  The master of the Sun and Sky,
And the creator of a neediness
  Only he could satisfy.

But his readers liked the news-sheets,
  How they loved his cheeky style.
They didn't know about his methods
  And his treachery and guile.

For years the Sun kept shining
  And outsold all the rest.
So great Count Titticumcum
  Felt that he'd been blessed.

But success can turn to hubris.
  And in time the darker side
Of the empire's operations
  Undermined its lusty pride.

Some realised their hacks were hacking
  Where hacks should never tread.
The empire's edifice was cracking!
  But who'd been in its bed?

Well, they ordered an enquiry
  To uncover all the facts
Which revealed a vast corruption,
  A tangled web of sordid acts.

It transpired the mighty leader
  And the leader before him
Had both courted Titticumcum!
  Oh, how horrible! How grim!

The News Lord of the World was shaken!
  So he espoused a deep regret
As his empire seemed in trouble.
  Was the Sun about to set?

Though the wicked witch denied it,
  As did her big bad boss
In the end they couldn't hide it,
  Though they didn't give a toss

About the people they had slandered
  And the awful things they'd done
For they felt they were almighty
  As controllers of the Sun.

But Time is the great healer.
  And as the count owned that as well
He was able to continue
  To dispense his sunny spell.

And though Count Titticumcum
  Still controls his great empire
The wicked witch was sacrificed
  Into the media's fire.

For when bad deeds are uncovered
  Someone has to pay the toll.
So to protect the big head at the top
  The red head had to roll.

(The best stories have no ending.
  They just pause... then start again.
And great Count Titticumcum
  Continues still to reign.)

Syrian Tragedy: the thoughts of President Assad

Bury the dead
Carry on as before
Say to the world there is no civil war
It worked for my father
It will work for me
It's written in blood so let the blood be

Bury the dead
There's more death in store
Don't open the crack to democracy's door
I am the dictator
Brutal and strong
There is no one greater, I'll go on and on

Shoot the insurgents
But don't keep the score
If we shoot enough they won't come back for more
Don't give them an inch
Or they'll take a mile
I will survive by cunning and guile

The Russians are with us
Let's ignore the rest
All they can do is protest and protest
Bring on the peace envoys
Show them around
After the blood has been washed from the ground

Squash the insurgents
Bring out the tanks
To leave a few holes in their scurrilous ranks
Then bury the dead
Carry on as before
We will not give in, we will win this war

Cast in Stone

"All the great masterful races have been fighting races."
Theodore Roosevelt

From the Stone Age to the Stoned Age
Man has worshipped gods of war
Someone will cast the first stone
That's the nature of Man's flaw
From our birth until our old age
We will fight and we will squabble
As we manifest our road rage
To fuel our need for trouble

From the first page to the last page
Of the stories from our past
From the first stage to the last stage
Those old enmities will last
From the tribal to the lone age
From the cradle to the grave
To the modern mobile phone age
For the free man and the slave

There's a drumbeat in our heartbeat
That compels us to compete
There's aggression in that pounding
That makes a man complete
We must do it unto others
Before they do it unto us
And so we slay our brothers
In the heat of our blood-lust

In war cemeteries white sentinels
Remind us of the dead
And the poets have recalled the lies
The dead ones had been fed
Wilfred Owen and his classmates
Commemorated in their verse
The horror of war's stalemates
And the nature of Man's curse

It's the curse that we were born with
That no nation claims it owns
It recurs in every story
Breaking hearts and breaking bones
It is etched upon our hard drive
It's infused into our soul
From the Stone Age to the Stoned Age
Our truth is cast in stone

Thanks firstly to my editor Sally Britton who has worked tirelessly to review and organise this work. Thanks also to Richard Bradley for his proof-reading and valued feedback. And thanks to everyone who has bought my books or attended my events and inspired me to sustain my efforts.

I hope you have enjoyed reading this book as much as I enjoyed writing it. Check out my website for events and further information or email me.

www.windmillbard.co.uk
windmillbard@aol.co.uk

T G Carter